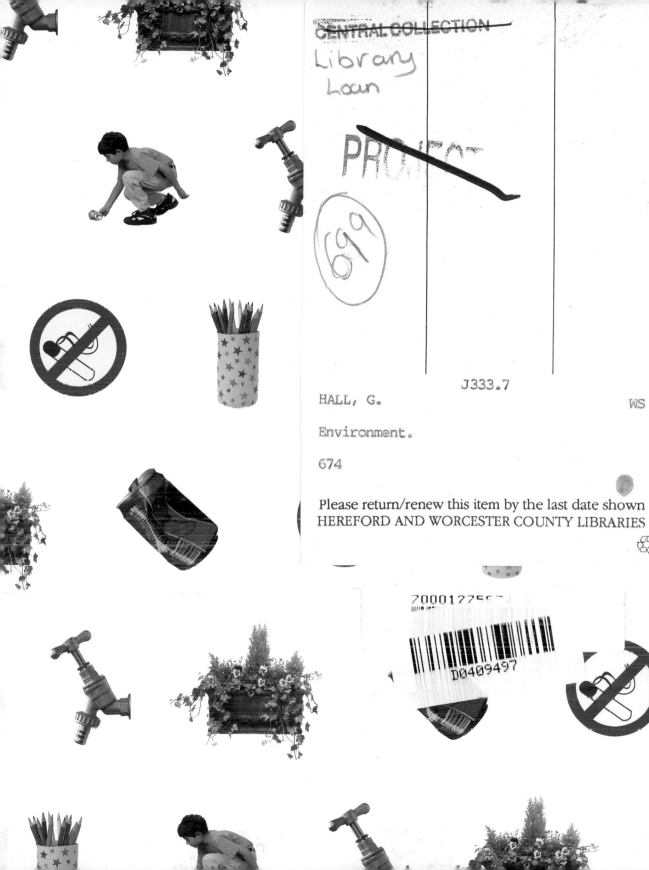

FIND OUT ABOUT

environment

Godfrey Hall

BBC

© **Godfrey Hall / BBC Education 1995**

BBC Education
201 Wood Lane
London W12 7TS

ISBN 0 563 39620 2

Editor: Debbie Reid
Designer: Peter Shirtcliffe
Picture research: Helen Taylor
Educational advisers: Samina Miller and Shelagh Scarborough
Photographer: John Green

With grateful thanks to: Rebecca Ingrey, Junior Varma, The National Asthma Campaign, RECOUP, Thames Water and Walt Disney Company

Researched photographs © Bossu/Sygma (page 7); Bruce Coleman Ltd (pages 4, 5 left, 6, 8, 11, 12 and 21); Ecoscene/Sally Morgan (page 13); Environmental Picture Library (page 14 bottom left); NHPA (page 9); Planet Earth Pictures (page 5 right); Tony Stone Images (page 10)

Printed in Belgium by Proost

Contents

A **moth**, an **owl**, a **squirrel** and **fungi** can all live together in one place.

What is an environment?

An environment provides the things that all living creatures need to live. Animals and plants need air to breathe. They also need food and water to live.

Plants, animals and insects can live together in one place. This could be in a tree or in a wood.

Some plants and animals live in damp, dark places. Some plants and animals live in hot, dry places. Other plants and animals can live in water.

cactus

seaweed

When a tree is chopped down, a **stump** is left. **Insects** and **animals** can live in the stump. There is also room for **new plants** to grow.

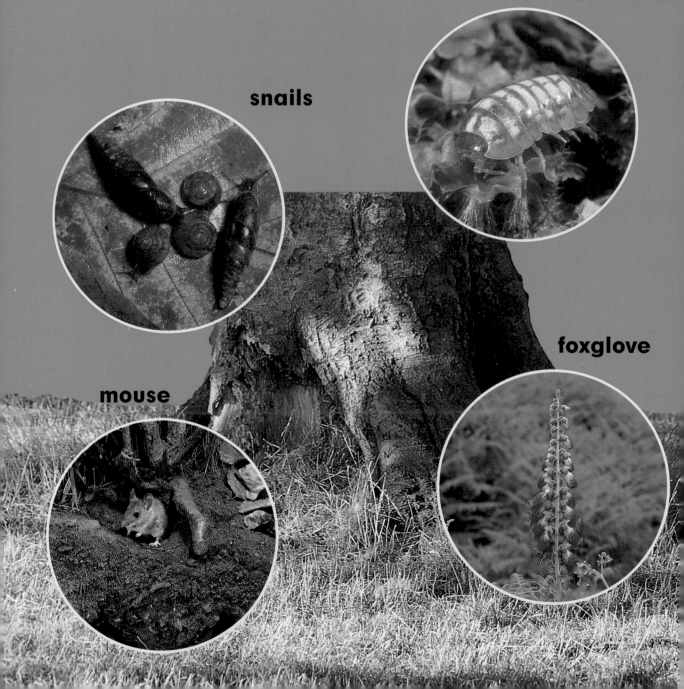

wood louse

snails

foxglove

mouse

What happens when we change things?

It is important that we do not try to change the way plants, animals and insects live.

When a tree is chopped down, it may die. The plants and animals living there have to move away. They have to find new homes.

But there can be good changes. The tree that has been chopped down can now make room for young trees to grow. Fungi and moss may grow on the stump of the tree. More insects may come and live on it.

Trees may also die from **acid rain**. This happens when **pollution** mixes with raindrops and falls on the trees.

This is a
food chain.

fish

insect

people

plant

Why do animals and plants live together?

Animals must eat if they are to live. Many animals feed on plants. They live close to plants so that they can find food easily.

Some animals eat plants and other animals. A bird can eat fish. Insects can eat other insects.

In a pond or river, insects eat the plants. Fish and other animals eat these insects. We eat the fish and animals. This is called a food chain.

There are even plants that eat insects.

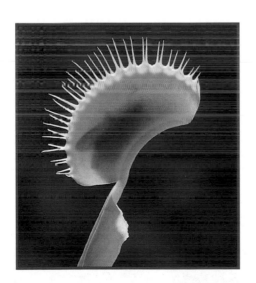

This plant is called a **Venus Flytrap.** Can you see the **fly** which has been **trapped** inside?

This **penguin chick** keeps **warm** against its parent's **body**.

Penguins' **feathers** are **thick** and keep out water. This helps them to stay **warm** and **dry**.

How can animals live in different places?

Animals and plants can live in very cold places or very hot places. They all need different things to live there.

Animals that live in very cold places have layers of fur or feathers to keep them warm. In the Antarctic, penguins have oily feathers to keep out the cold and wet.

In hot places, the animals and plants are very different. Some animals have large ears to keep them cool. During the day, some animals live below the sand. They come out at night when it is cooler.

The **jack rabbit** lives in the desert. Its **large ears** help to keep it **cool**. It also get **shade** from rocks and shrubs.

Foxes can live in the **countryside**. They **eat small animals, insects, birds, worms, fruit** and **vegetables**.

Sometimes foxes can live in **towns** and **cities**. They can get their food from **scraps** in dustbins.

How do plants and animals find new homes?

As we build new houses and shops, we use up more of our countryside. Many of the animals and insects have to find new places to live. To do this they have to change.

Foxes usually live in the countryside. They can now be found living in towns and cities.

In cities and towns, waste land is being made into wild areas. Old railway lines are being turned into footpaths. Plants, animals and insects can live here.

This **footpath** used to be a **railway line.** Can you see the old signal?

Water from the **tap** . . .

. . . goes down the **plug hole** and into a **pipe** . . .

. . . and ends up at the **sewage farm.**

The **clean water** goes back into our **rivers** and **seas**.

. . . it travels through the pipe and into a **drain** outside . . . it then goes into a **sewer pipe** underground . . .

What happens to our water?

When we finish having a bath or washing our hands, we pull out the plug. The water disappears down the plug hole. But where does it go?

Once it leaves the sink or bath it travels through pipes into a sewer pipe underground. The sewer pipe collects all the waste water. This water travels through the pipes to a sewage farm. Here the dirt and germs are taken out. The water then returns to our rivers and seas.

We should **never waste** water. We need it for **drinking** and **keeping clean**. It is important to use it **carefully**.

Chimneys can make the **air dirty** with their **smoke.**

The smoke and fumes **stay** in the air. This makes it harder to **breathe**.

Dirty fumes can also come from **cars** and **buses.**

Why should we look after our air?

Plants and animals need air to live. It is important that we look after it and try to keep it clean.

Lots of our air today is dirty. Cars and buses make the air dirty with their fumes. Factories can make the air dirty with smoke. Many buildings turn black because of smoke and fumes.

We can all help keep our air clean. We can ride a bicycle instead of driving a car. We can ask people not to smoke.

Some people can become **ill** if they breathe in dirty air. They have to use **inhalers.**

no-smoking sign

This bag is made of **plastic.**

This bottle is made of **glass.**

This can is made of **aluminium.**

These peelings have come from **potatoes** and **carrots.**

What **other** types of **rubbish** can you think of?

How can we sort our rubbish?

We throw away lots of rubbish. If you could put your own rubbish into your bedroom, it would soon cover the floor.

Bins are full of different types of rubbish. The things we throw away are made of different materials. Cereal boxes are made of cardboard. Fizzy drinks bottles can be made of plastic or glass.

We can sort our rubbish into glass, card, paper, plastic, metal, clothes and food scraps. Some things can be used again, but some cannot.

Make your own pencil holder!

Wash out a washing-up liquid bottle.

Ask an adult to cut off the top.

Paint or decorate it. Use it for keeping pencils in.

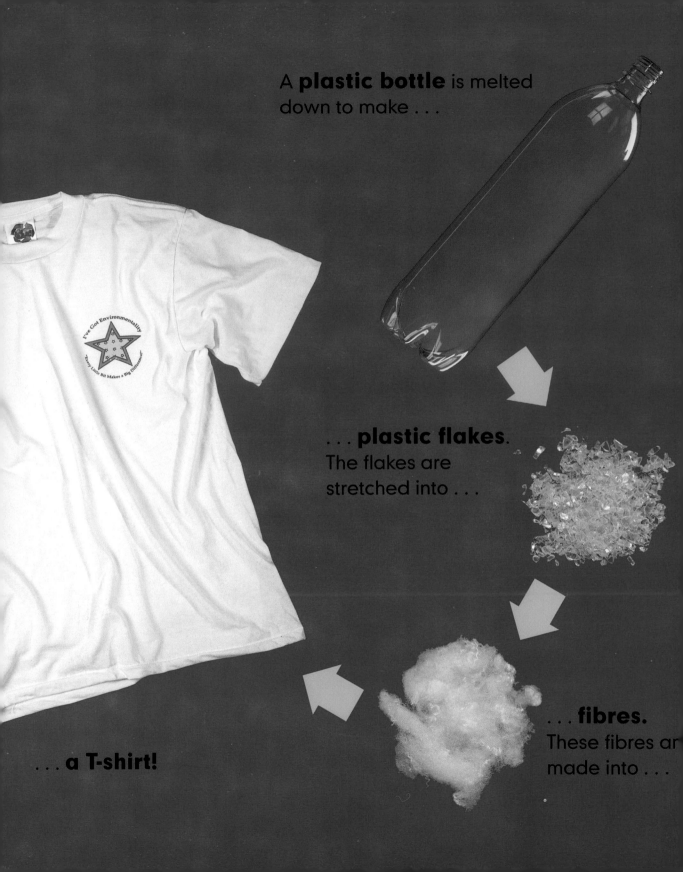

A **plastic bottle** is melted down to make . . .

. . . **plastic flakes**. The flakes are stretched into . . .

. . . **fibres**. These fibres are made into . . .

. . . **a T-shirt!**

What is recycling?

Many everyday things can be changed and turned into something completely different. This is called recycling.

Glass bottles are melted down. They are turned into new glass. Cans are turned into new metal. Old paper is used to make new paper. Plastic bottles can even be turned into T-shirts!

Around the country there are special places where people can take their used bottles, paper and cans. These are taken away to recycling plants. Here the old glass, paper and cans are turned into other things.

Plastic bottles are collected . . . and sorted for recycling.

Flowers are grown in **window boxes**. These can attract insects like bees and butterflies.

We can try to keep the environment **clean!**

How can we make our environment better?

We can try to make our environment cleaner and safer. We can encourage birds and insects into our cities. Some people grow colourful plants in their gardens or window boxes. These plants can attract bees and butterflies.

We should not throw litter on the streets. This can be dangerous to small animals and birds. If we have any litter, we should put it into a bin or take it home with us.

Warning: Always be careful when picking up litter. Wear gloves if you have them and remember to wash your hands afterwards!

Index

~~~~~~